James Thomson Callender

Letters to Alexander Hamilton

King of the Feds

James Thomson Callender

Letters to Alexander Hamilton
King of the Feds

ISBN/EAN: 9783337877644

Printed in Europe, USA, Canada, Australia, Japan

Cover: Foto ©Thomas Meinert / pixelio.de

More available books at **www.hansebooks.com**

LETTERS

TO

ALEXANDER HAMILTON,

KING OF THE FEDS.

NEW YORK:

PRINTED FOR THE HAMILTON CLUB.

1866.

7
.

LETTERS

TO

ALEXANDER HAMILTON,

𝕶ing of the 𝕱eds.

CI-DEVANT SECRETARY OF THE TREASURY

OF THE

UNITED STATES OF AMERICA,

INSPECTOR-GENERAL OF THE *STANDING* ARMIES

THEREOF,

COUNSELLOR AT LAW.

&c. &c. &c.

Being intended as a reply to a SCANDALOUS PAMPHLET lately publifhed under the fanction, as it is pre-fumed, of Mr. Hamilton, and figned with the fignature of JUNIUS PHILÆNUS.

BY TOM CALLENDER, ESQ.
CITIZEN OF THE WORLD.

—NEW-YORK:—
PRINTED BY RICHARD REYNOLDS, No. 27, DEY-STREET.

1802.

LETTER THE FIRST.

ALEXANDER HAMILTON,

———————

"MENE MENE, TEKEL UPHARSIN."

DAN. v. 25.

MR. HAMILTON, for you are no more commander
in chief of the Pittsburgh army, the motto quoted
above from a good old book, although it may not at
present be exactly applicable to you, or your former
friend Mr. Adams, was once the very game you both
played! Start not, Sir! your nerves are strong and
able to bear up a great weight of *any kind.* You
have disavowed being the patron of the licentiousness
of the press, and yet you have made more use of that

Instrumentality to carry on intrigues against the peace and happiness of the people than any other man in America!

THE pamphlet just published under the signature of JUNIUS PHILÆNUS, although it may have been written by some of the young fry belonging to the Bar, who are either your worshippers or slaves; nevertheless bears such evident symbols of your patronage that it is impossible for any man of common experience, not to see "the mark of the beast on its forehead."—The amanuensis, is too contemptible a *creature* for me to pursue, I therefore address myself to the principal and father of the bantling,— not so much on account of any injury that *that filthy Porcupiniade* could ever produce to the present peaceable administration, because it is a weak and silly performance which must defeat its own purpose; not on account of any any injury you or the Jersy-Jove, the apostate Luther Martin, the vulgar Pickerings and Wolcotts, the Harpooners, Burrs or Brutuses, &c. could effect. None of those reasons or fears have operated upon me, to provoke me into revenge against any of the whole corps of YE. It is the disturbance which ye are continually raising up against the public tranquillity!—I am happy that we now all live at peace in this country and that men of wealth are well secured in their property, without having recourse to the blood thirsty plans of burning villages, as it is reported, you had declared, and I believe with great truth, you would have put into operation, if you could only have provoked any of the insurgents to shoot a single man of the militia or volunteers who marched out, in my opinion, with the utmost honor and spirit, to quell an innovation against the laws of the United States, but never. oh never, had they collectively any such horrid idea as that of staining their hands in the blood of their fellow-citizens without discrimination!—I have been told of this your declaration, so often that I was almost convinced it was true. But let me here declare to you, that, at this day, I have strong doubts of its veracity, and I wish you could deny it unequivocally—*that you presumed to take a vow like Hannibal,* "THEY (your confidants,) should either see you returning at the head of a triumphant army or see you without a head!" I don't know before what altar you could have made so desperate an oath?—Nor am I inclined to give it credence, because I am not, nor ever have been, your personal enemy. If, however, in the result it should appear, that you really did use such an expression; there will remain little doubt in my mind, of your having " fostered," in the language of your friend Asmodeus of Morrisania, an hope, of what? of crushing down the spirit of republicanism by FORCE OF ARMS! The God of nature was disgusted with the brutal purpose, and although you have enlisted a few respectable gentlemen of the pulpit to write in favor of your systems—those defenders of your faith will soon forsake you.—Let them look at my motto—let them read over the fourth and fifth chapters of Daniel— and confess that they are very applicable to yours and John Adams's administrations, for we know, that the great and good Washington was liable to be imposed on by both of ye; let those political preachers consider the fate of BELTESHAZZAR, and then confess whether the death he brought upon himself was not just and merciful, considering the crimes he had committed! His fall was sudden and great—and so has been the fall of the Monarchical party in the United States. They attempted to set us all at war with one another. To tax us as cruelly as the Jews were by the Egyptians, to put gags in our mouths, so that we dared not to open our lips in the War-Office or Treasury, or Custom-Houses of America! least some half a dozen upstart clerks and informers should bear false witness against us and bring us up to the *bull-ring* of persecution.

THOSE were hard times, Mr. Hamilton, and although perhaps you did not directly sanction such illiberality; I have seen you smiling with pleasure at the heart-scalding effects it produced; even amongst some of your own old friends and comparitots in war. How could you smile at the honest complaints of a good old whig?—I shall never allow any man in my presence to say that you are dishonest; but surely you have exposed yourself, as being the monument that enclosed a living spirit of destruction to the wealth and prosperity of all America.

THIS may appear to some of your friends, to be rather an harsh expression, yet tt is my intention to endeavour to prove it to be founded in truth, as I *" expect"* to do, in the phrase of one of your satellites (Wolcott) in the course of this correspondence.

THE schism that has been attempted to be set on foot by the Vice-President, amongst the republicans, is a thing totally beneath my notice, because it will die and rot of its own corruption, and we shall have no more of those cloudy days of terror which disgraced the late administration, but still I can not suffer myself to believe that you could prostitute your talents to sanction that disgraceful system. You certainly must have a proper respect for the character that is to be estimated of you by the children of futurity. But the schism attempted by Burr, although it is despicable in my eyes, as is the founders of it —still leaves a doubt behind, that you either know something of its origin, or, after a time, you must have suffered yourself to approve of the plot—I hope not.—It is for reasons like these, and they are far from chimerical; that I am obliged to view you in the light of a very desperate and dangerous enemy to society, although I am ready to join in the general approbation of your valuable abilities, and your *abstemiousness* from all pecuniary considerations and all other sublunary *things!*

I do not mean to hurt your *private* feelings, but only to make some general observations upon your political career, from its Alpha to its *Omega, which* I think must now be fast approaching, from your connection with so scurrilous a wretch as he who could have penned the pamphlet subscribed by master *Junius Philænus*, whose insolence is equal to his ignorance, whose connection with you must be disgraceful—whose Billingsgate style is lower than even the brutal British-Porcupine—But he shall be dissected in my next letter, or some other letter in this series, which I have sat down to write for no other reason than the defence of truth, honor, virtue, and real patriotism; unsophisticated patriotism.—Unlike your complicated schemes.—Unlike Adams's dreams.—Unlike Duer's financial operations, which you had the folly to father.

THE very lengthy introductory-apology which prefaces master Philænus's pamphlet, was not,—no, never, written by the same hand that afterwards sinks into the lowest filth of sweep-chimney's dialect.— His debut, however, is perhaps intended to shew us that he is a *sportsman,* by the use of the word "*Bevy* of hungry expectants." Of which number he *vows* in Yankee phrase, that he's not one, HE *himself*—who has taken up so many pages to define his own *excellence*—he never was an expectant for any office, nor would he accept of one were it to be offered to him, let it be ever so lucrative?—As well might Oliver Wolcott publish to the world the barefaced assertion, that he himself was the entire and sole author of a lame defence, lately published, of the late administration;—or have the effrontery to tell the people of the United States, that he did not come to New-York to get it corrected and amended by the centre flugel-man of all mischief,—who is still the rallying point for the out-casts of republicanism

—whose meetings, Cacusses, plots, and stratagems, are not so secret as the junto may vainly imagine.

THEIR frequent intrigues at New-York will never be construed into innocent visits of private friendship.—*The Jersey-Jove's races* through the three middle states are not all probably intended as visits of personal respect to the *fallen angels* of an intended royal standard—neither did Luther Martin, and many others whom I may probably make mention of hereafter, all come here to New-York for nothing?—Have not you Mr. Hamilton, expressed yourself in a very treasonable style at the town-meetings amongst the Cartmen or the Shoe-makers—something about dictating to the President of the United States whatever laws and regulations you pleased? By what means? By stirring up a sort of rebellion in the eastern states!

SHALL we not have the freedom of election allowed us to choose a good and virtuous man for our President?—Would you and Dayton have dragooned us out of our right of suffrage?—You have always arrogated too much DOMINION to yourself, over the minds of men.—You were not pleased with the INSPIRED WASHINGTON, for I will call him such, for our commander in chief. You said, as I was told, from the lips of General Malcom, " that Washington was totally unequal to the task of commanding the revolutionary armies; and that there was none of the officers excepting General Greene, qualified for that duty." Sir—no man will deny the great and noble virtues of YOUR FAVORITE; but, when you presumed to depreciate the talents of the virtuous hero of his country, you added no laurels to the brows of Greene: —all-hallowed be the memory of each of them.

As to your own merits and services, they would have been handed down to posterity with their just approbation had you stuck by the good old cause of republicanism, but when we saw you so soon after the revolution shooting yourself like a tangent into the atmosphere of monarchy, and attempting to impose it on the people under false colours—by calling it federalism when you knew very well it was no more than a stepping stone toward tyranny—when we considered all the dark intrigues and deep-laid plots of your party flowing on so fast, like a tide of destruction, to overwhelm us!—it was then high time to stem the torrent, and it has happily been effected—by the removal of you and your dangerous army of informers, speculators, and dragooners of the people, from the high stations ye held over the affairs of this now happy country, which never was secured before in the blessings of peace and good government. That you all have acknowledged the federal constitution to be no more than a sham to introduce a monarchy, is well known by the various speeches and essays of Mr. Adams and many others and even by the young confidant, Fenno, who published his marplot pamphlet entitled " DESULTORY OBSERVATIONS," on the affairs of the United States.

THE fall which your party has experienced was therefore no more than you deserved, and I believe as justly inflicted on ye, as the punishment of Belteshazzer, as mentioned in my motto. The people are at length satisfied with the tranquility and prosperity that surrounds them, they can sleep in peace without being terrified with the shouts of warriors.—They are

not betrayed by spies—they enjoy the light of heaven
without being insulted and imprisoned by excise-men
—they can transact their commercial and other relations without going to a stamp-office &c. But you
will not permit us to live in this tranquility and happiness.—The disbanded few, who have lost their consequence, are everlastingly trumping up some infamous falsehood in the news-papers, in pamphlets
and in treasonable night *Caucusses*, which it is certain are frequently held in New-York, and in the
management of which societies, it is strongly sus-
pected you are a principal. The pamphlet now before
me, of *Junius Philænus*, is a *handsome* specimen of the
malignity of the men who encouraged its publication,
and if you Sir, were of the number it will never redound to your fame or character. The world has
never yet heard from Mr. Jefferson, the real causes of
many of the removals he has been obliged to make.
It was lord chief justice Mansfield's opinion that a
man at the head of a public office should never give
his reasons for the removal of those who should render
themselves deserving of it—and who knows what

proofs, what complaints, what letters and strong vouchers, may have been laid before Mr. Jefferson, of the ill conduct of many of those who have lost the confidence of the administration—Yet they will not rest quiet under their imaginary disgrace, but for ever keep up a fire of slander against him. It would be better for their own sakes they would be silent, as, if the President should be urged to publish the reasons of *some* of their removals, it would, perhaps, only add to their chagrin—better for them to remain contented with the simple punishment of removal, than have the complicated disgrace of their characters being also exposed. There never was so great a crowd of public offices filled by men who were *every one immaculate!*—Humanity is liable to error. The countenance and support which, I am convinced, you give to the EVENING POST, and to most of the same description of scandalous prints, as well as the encouragement to such reptiles as *Junius Philænus,* is so disgusting to the true friends of America, that you have drawn down their indignation upon yourself. You have deserted the cause of genuine republicanism, and fled to the standard of Aristocracy. You held a post of high rank among the Duke of Braintree's WELL-BORN sons, until you were almost ashamed of it and him. Your letter, addressed to him, is sufficient for me to believe that you most heartily despised him.—But, your enmity against the present Administration, proceeds from very different motives. You do not—you cannot look with the same degree of contempt on the abilities and virtues of Mr. JEFFERSON with which you viewed the weakness and vanity of Mr. Adams. Your pretended disapprobation of the President's conduct, is only external; for, I will pay you the compliment to say, that I sincerely believe your heart approves of it. The chief objection to him is the displacing of some men who could not,—would not, concur with the salutary and absolutely necessary measures that he has adopted for the preservation of the government. Suppose Sir, that you were, for instance, elevated to the Presidential chair, and were to be made acquainted with some mal-practices in the various departments of the administration—would you not remove those men from office whom you should find to be guilty? I must think you certainly would. And yet there are many of this description who still hold their places under Mr. Jefferson ; because, perhaps, he does not yet know their faults—Suppose Sir, you, as President of the United States, were to be substantially convinced in the most unequivocal manner, that any officer of considerable consequence, with a good fat salary, should live so dissipated a life as to be obliged to borrow money from all his industrious neighbours to support his extravagance, nay even to obtain it in a surreptitious manner from a merchant, under the cloak of his office—he should apply it to his own private use, and leave the merchant afterwards to pay it over again—and after all this shameful transaction, this officer should refuse to refund the money or secure it—but suffer himself to be exposed by a suit in the Mayor's court, which he put off as long as the court would permit his lawyers to do it; and, finally, when the merchant was on the point of getting out an execution, he was astonished to find the cause was removed into another court. I say Mr. Hamilton, if you were President of the United States

3

would you not remove this officer from your confidence? I am sure you would.

But Sir. this is only one instance out of many which might be mentioned to shew that the President is in possession of sufficient information to induce him to act as he has done; and that, so far from treating those discarded gentlemen with cruelty, he keeps their faults secret, which is the mildest method he could have adopted. For the proof of the above fact, I need only refer you to the records of the courts, and to the information of one of your most intimate friends at the bar.—*Verbum sat.*

Now, let me ask my fellow-citizens, whether our public affairs are not now lodged in safer hands than they would have been, had the people suffered them to remain in the hands of men of such characters as I have described—is not the monied and the landed interests of the country as safe in the hands of our present happy administration, as it could have been under the government of the former rulers—have we not, *at least*, as good security for the honor of our wives and daughters

Your amorous transactions I will not hint at in these letters, unless some of the scribbling fools should provoke me to it by using such low indelicate innuendos as the pamphlet now alluded to is stuffed with. Desperate indeed must be the situation of that *faction* who would hire such scurrillous scribblers. It has been said of the people of Connecticut, that they had for the last three or four years, taken the SHINE of dissimulation from every other state or nation—the poor Irish not excepted. But the whole state of Connecticut cannot produce half a dozen such *creditable gentlemen* as have broken into this country, within a few years from Caledonia. *Take notice*, Sir, I mean no reflection on that country in general, because I circulate some Scotch blood, as probably may be the case with yourself. I now confine my remarks to *the* Callender at Richmond, and John Wood, lately of New-York, who have been so kindly received into the monarchical club—Mr. Wood is really a *valuable acquisition* to any society—he is teacher of half a dozen languages, none of which can he speak or write!—if this be not presumption, I know not where imper-

tinence will end. One day, like Mr. Lang, on the
French negro-landing, he tells truth by affirming to
the world that he is a liar, and the next he asserts
that he was a liar when he told the the truth!—yet this
is the man who has had the assurance to undertake
to write upon religion, and government—WHO WILL
BELIEVE HIM?—what an handsome importation it was
when we hail'd him and the *wheel-barrow* man to our
shores? neither of them could know any thing of the
true interests of America. But they will try their
hands, also, at book-making.   Every cow-boy in Scot-
land attempts to become an author, and with the effrontery of Belzebub they will venture neck and limb
on writing a book; and when they are found out afterwards to be nothing better than common plagiarists
and impostors, their character stands in as good a situation as it was before.   They lose nothing, and they
gain notoriety, much in the same way that the famous
Guy Faux did, and it is to be hoped they may meet
with a similar *reward*.   In making this observation,
I must repeat my former declaration, that I mean to
make no allusion or reflection upon that country

which has produced so many men of as great abilities and virtue as any nation whatever.

THIS most disgraceful and unnatural enlistment of Wood and Calendar into the monarchial-federal corps can never aid or assist to raise up those men who have justly lost their consequence in the eyes of the public; but who are striving hard to deceive about five millions of sensible people into the idea, THAT THEY,—the discomfited, and discarded few—are the ONLY MEN fitted to hold the reins of government.— Was it not right and wise to snatch the whips from their hands? Such desperate men as these are would now wade up to their necks in blood to recover their former stations, and like Milton's Prince of the power of foul airs, they would rebel against any government let it be ever so well administered, unless THEY were to be the supreme dictators. No wonder that the people of such an enlightened Country as ours, should take the reins, the whips and the spurs away from those Jehus. And if THEY should EVER recover them again, it must happen in consequence of some extra-ordinary anodynes being treacherously administered to lull the people into a profound sleep, whilst THEY were Paoli-ing them.   It is not THEIR abilities, either as writers, painters, politicians, printers, or soldiers,— that can give them a superior title to the confidence of mankind—because, we have always experienced the superior powers of the republican spirit whenever they were forced or provoked to exert it.   And so it will be for ever more, AMEN.

In my next letter, I shall probably take some notice of your hopeful young scribe Philænus—But lest I should tire you too much at the first onset, I will here make a PAUSE!—in the borrowed language of your friend Asmodeus, who conceited himself, no doubt, a second Cicero, (as I may call myself a second Daniel) for "you have been weighed in the balance, and found wanting"—and your *dominion* over the government of the United States shall be taken from you and divided amongst the old whigs and republicans.

TOM CALLENDER.

LETTER II.

Sir,

" IN addressing you," saith your young scriblerus, "I AM NOT ACTUATED by any of *those motives* which have gathered around you such a BEVY of hungry expectants," &c. In conformity to the plan attempted by him, the said amanuensis, I can safely say, that, neither am I actuated by any such motives:—nor shall my respect for Mr. Hamilton's literary abilities, intimidate me into the submissive stile of PHILÆNUS, who takes up five and twenty pages of his pamphlet about himself and his wonderful acquirements, and political and religious tenets. On the contrary, I will make no apology to the public for writing these letters to you Sir, whom I have always considered as the greatest Machiavel in America, although I never thought you were the GREATEST man.

This was the opinion of Bishop Talleyrand: That thou wert the Saviour of this happy land. But whether the bishop did or did not express those sentiments to *Doctor* Smith, of South Carolina, over a bottle of wine, is a query of little consequence to the world ; as William Smith's character has been tolerably well defined by Doctor Ramsey, to whoever will take the trouble to look into the Charlestown news-papers at the time of their contested election.

The high-flowing stile of yourself which only obscures the understanding without convincing it, I shall not attempt upon the good sense of my fellow-citizens, neither will I box the compass of dictionaryship like messieurs Webster, Coleman, Philænus, and Co. to steal language of which they were never originally possessed. I say Sir, I mean not to ape your lofty stile, nor mimic the low cant of Coleman and Callender —one of whom, (the *new ally* of the Hamiltonian-dominion,) is my *name-sake*, although he is no blood-relation; because he himself told me, that he was greatly afflicted with a weakness of the nerves, a disorder with which none of my family of the Callenders have ever been pestered. As an instance of this, and lest any of yours or the Vice-President's friends and gladiators should imagine that I was any way bashful about naming the Revenue officer whom I have hinted at in my first letter, I here beg leave to refer to Mr. Troup who brought the suit against him, and if he should hesitate on the business, I can appeal to the merchant, who will substantiate the fact, and who told me, he was resolved to lay the state of his case before the President of the United States.—You may perceive that I go upon good ground; and it must appear evident to your superior intellect, that although there may be one man in America who would use *second*-means to get rid of a rival, I dread him not. But, with respect to you, Sir, I declare, that, so far from suspecting you of countenancing so base a proceeding, I am heartily convinced of your strict adherence to the principles of a soldier and a man, and that you would detest any wretch that would implicate upon himself such a vile suspicion.

I think it necessary to make this declaration of my private opinion of you as a gentleman, though I may widely differ with you in general politics. From you, I am confident, I am perfectly secure, with respect to any foul mode of resentment; but, Sir, I do not consider ALL your allies in the same honorable point of

4

of view. After the dark-handed conspiracy of a certain conceited lawyer, who, to get rid of an opponent, would use adventitious means, it is high time for the genuine friends of America to look sharp. If such men as these were to rule the roast, we should soon witness the death of the liberties and prosperity of America. The literary assassin is, undoubtedly, a great pest to society; but the savages who undertake to bully voters at times of election, or, indeed, at any other time, should be marked, and I have so minutely watched their conduct as to be able to develope most of their secret intrigues for the attainment of power. The base and cowardly attacks made upon republican printers at New-York, Philadelphia, and other parts of the United States, will not soon be forgotten. The circumstance of Duane's being held fast by one of the strongest men in America, whilst the son of a conservator of our laws played off the *valour* of his fists upon his face, is such an instance of turpitude, as, I hope, I shall never hear of an equal to; nor shall I easily forgive Duane for not having taken an exemplary revenge. It is true he challenged the youth, who it is

generally allowed, modestly refused to meet him. The
Democrats may here suppose I am not altogether up
to their systems—nor am I.—Neither did I ever consider the magistrate alluded to, nor his secretary Dal-
las, nor Ingersoll, who is intended for the next governor, as true republicans. I could here give my
reasons, but I leave the decision to such men as have
been in habits of intimacy with them. In the same
light do I view some leading characters in the states
of New-York, Jersey, &c. Mr. Bloomfield is no republican—neither art thou, Mr. Hamilton, notwithstanding your opposition to the Duke of Braintree's chimerical monarchy. You will here naturally observe
that I am not amongst the list of timid scribblers—
not very much alarmed at the resentment of disap-
pointed royalists—or the furious thunder bolts of
brother Jonathan. For if, they attack me in front I
will endeavor to defend myself as well as I can—and
if they take me in the rear—I am sure it will not be
with your consent.

THE sportsman-like phrase of Philænus at the onset
of his pamphlet might induce some honest fellows of

the chace to follow him through the forest; but if any of them should give a view-holla, he will not come up within a mile of the hunt—and so far from being calculated for a huntsman, he is incapable of performing the duty of a whipper-inn to a pack of well trained *harriers.*

On purchasing the pamphlet, I carelessly opened it at page 48, and on reading lines 5, 6, 7 and 8 could not restrain a laugh at master Philænus's sagacious remarks on the conduct of Mr. Jefferson. He accuses the President, of having expressed "his contempt for their (the members of the late ejection) understandings, by answering their reasonable and respectful remonstrances with a pompous display of *logical nonsense* and angry recriminations."—Who is there amongst the sons of the monarchical-feds that can explain to us the meaning of logical nonsense? Stop the youth from writing, as soon as possible; otherwise he will put an extinguisher over the dying flames of aristocracy. It is really wasting time to look over this poor pamphlet. Nor would any one think of doing it, were it not for the general conviction that Mr. Hamilton approved of its publication. Sir, why will you not suffer an experiment to be made in the art of simplifying government under the management of Mr. Jefferson; as you desired when you led the van under the administration of the great and good, but much imposed on Washington, with your complicated plans? —all you asked from the opposition then, was to give them a fair trial;—which was consented to; and not only your plans, but your language and your pen were allowed too great a range of absolute licentiousness. Your party in New-York were ready not only to support you with their purses but even to mob any man in the streets who differed in opinion with themselves and you.

The result has been, as I have already said, in conformity with my text—your dominion has been taken from you, &c. by the general consent and will of the people on whom you calculated to enforce your schemes by threatenings and hard blows.

The various systems of intrigue carried on, by your associates, at that time, are fresh in my recollection. The attempt made by a private citizen, when in Eu-

rope, at the time of the debate upon your funding
system, to purchase the whole debt which the United
States owed to France. and to sell this contract to the
Hopes of Amsterdam, who were to furnish the money,
was a subject in the senate, who rejected the nomina-
tion of that citizen, by the President, to the place of
ambassador to France; yet he was afterwards appointed, through the intrigues of Robert Morris, whose
relation to him was no more than being concerned in
a plan for selling lands in the moon, to European
speculators, which, when properly enquired for, were
not to be found. Hence the depreciation of the American character in Europe originated, and hence the
subsequent reduction of the financier-general of the
United States, to the humble station of a birth in the
jail of Philadelphia. If he had only considered the
old saying, "that honesty is the best policy." He
never would have consented to be concerned with this
Diable Boiteaux, who ruined his credit and consequence
in Europe. Perhaps it was from this circumstance
that John Adams took up the idea which he has so
patriotically expressed in the book he wrote in London,

yclept "*A Defence of the American Constitution,*"
wherein he says, that the Americans "have no character." Thank you Mr. Adams—you were then probably in the same way of thinking that the Diable
Boiteaux expressed lately in the Senate of the United
States when he said the people themselves were their
own worst enemies? what an elegant figure in rheto-
ric was this to come from the lips of such a Cicero?
—It was kind, and merciful, indeed, when bellowed
from the lungs of a man of the most contracted abilities amongst the feds, but of the most unlimited
effrontery. His *hard*-earned estates, or fine house,
furniture, and equipage have not any effect upon the
real republicans to produce respect for his person or
his merit—I heartily despise both, and should pass an
evening with more genuine comfort in company with
a Poughkeepsie farmer, than with him and all his
bought or borrowed lustre. In the same estimation,
do I hold Mr. Bingham, the breeches-maker's son, at
Philadelphia. The trade, I hope, will not take offence
at my classing him amongst them. There are many
brokers in New-York, &c. who ride in coaches, but who

would appear more in character if they were to parade the streets in buttermilk-carts, or at the arms of bakers' wheelbarrows.

The vulgarity of some of the eastern members of Congress, is only to be equalled by their inclination to intrigue and low cunning. They *professed* the most unlimited obedience to your propositions, let them be ever so extravagant; yet when it came to voting for President of the U. States, &c. although you, Sir, had written a terrible letter against John Adams, as a private circular, to be first sent to the electors to influence them as far as your weight would carry it, and afterwards it was again published by Lang, in New-York, &c. The whole effect it had on the election, both in the Eastern and Southern states, was—That your letter did not make a single proselyte —nor did John Adams lose by it a single vote. From such experience as this, it is but fair to judge, that your interest and influence could effect nothing. The calling of caucausses, therefore, at New-York, of the discontented few, ought not to be considered, as any very dangerous combination against republicanism—

They, undoubtedly, were for an aristocracy. Adams was against them a little—he was for a monarchy; they could not agree, and republicanism came again out of the fire like pure gold.

THE particulars of these causes and effects I shall explain at not a very distant day,—nor shall any petty scribbler like Philænus prevent me. The intolerable use of detraction propagated by your associates, have brought down destruction on themselves—you shewed them an example in the phillippic you pronounced, long ago, against Washington, when you preferred Greene. You shewed them another example, in the same complimentary style, when you attempted to ridicule Gov. Clinton, in the letters you wrote for the Daily Advertiser in the years 1787-88, under the signature of H. G. The firs of those essays, on Washington, was no more than barking at the moon: and the second, against Clinton, had no better issue, altho' you put up Judge Yates, a good republican, against his friend—So it has been with you throughout your peregrinations in politics. They would have succeeded better, had they been grafted on a sounder stock—

your standing army, and excise, were equally ill-judged things. They might have answered for the next century, if our posterity should then become such abject tools to self-important architects of government as you and Mr. Adams. But Sir, government can, and has been simplified, as I have already said, and we find that republicanism may, can, and shall, be established. It would be well for you if you could agree with me in this sentiment. You are not so much tied down by your promises to aristocracy, but that you might make one more effort to regain your station amongst republicans. This may appear to some as a sly invitation to join the good old party; but, be assured, Sir, they generally think they can do very well without you.

You have had recourse to a vast quantity of *press-work*, and printing-offices in your time, to carry your points, let them be good or evil; and I remember when you were considered by the printers of New-York as inspector-general of every thing they should bring forth. Adieu to such days!———You must now stand on your own bottom, nor will all the Thunderer of

Jersey can do, forward you an inch in your designs.
I know not of any circumstance, plan, or scheme of
yours, that has been, in anywise likely to become permanent. Blame who you will for this defalcation,
I can scarcely imagine that it was altogether the child
of your own brain; let me rather suppose it was
vanity, like that by which Mr. Adams was actuated.
You had bad advisers, and they led you astray.

TOM CALLENDER.

LETTER III.

Sir,

SOME of your friends may pretend to say, it is un-
generous to attack you in print, as you are out of office, and have nothing to do with the present administration. This is true enough, you have not any
thing to do with it—in favour of it, or in support of
it—but you have something to do in the Rye-house-
plot-work that is brewing against it; which will
crumble to dust, as almost all your other political
plans have done.—We must and will have a quiet and

peaceable government—we have it now, and we will
keep it in despite of all the Macbeth witchcraft of the
fallen angels. You see I go freely into the *little* labour
of examining your GREAT works. The Pilot-boat man
makes *one* item of what you have to answer for. Your
winking at many improprieties committed against
the people's peace, as well as their pockets, is another!
and your countenancing the publication of such trash
as Junius Philœnus is a third, with many other thirds,
fifths, and octaves to fill up your concerto.

The finesse and stratagems which were practised on
Thomas Paine, by Robert Morris &c. in the years 1785,
and 1786, whilst he was at Philadelphia, are fresh in
my recollection. THEY (the enemies of American
commerce) ruined his character then, with his own
friends, by prevailing on him to write a pamphlet in
favour of the bank of North-America, which was composed of a set of traders, not bankers. They knew
nothing of banking. All the banks in Europe excepting the bank of England, are composed of men who
have CASH-capitals; none of your scrips will tell
there, because the banker is under an honorary obli-

gation not to interfere in any sort of merchandize—
he limits himself to the buying and selling of bullion.
But, in America, the banking gentry are all traders in
wet and dry goods; and when they want to speculate
upon a purchase of rum, sugar, or East India crockery,
they contrive to have a partner who sends his note to
the bank to be discounted, in order to provide the
means to make that very purchase : his friend amongst
the directors—his partner!—will certainly endeavour
to get *that* note done, in preference to a better note,
and a better man, and better security than the other.
Here is banking indeed, to reject good paper and take
in bad !

YOUR Philænus attempts to give us a balance-sheet
of the state of American affairs ; but let him, if he can,
explain to us the propriety of the above system ! On a
similar plan was the bank of the United States established :—It was pretended that it was to support the
government—and so it was. But what sort of a
government?—A government that was yet to be raised
upon the ruins of the present constitution, according
to any construction the Aristocrats might choose to

put upon it; and all this was to be effected by force of arms, and banks, and intrigue. Several unconstitutional acts were forced through the legislature, by small influenced majorities; and the power of the country, and the liberties of the people were about to be divided, like loaves and fishes, amongst about fifty or an hundred aristocrats.—Various orders of nobility were to be installed; and on the very day that Mr. Adams arrived at New-York to take the chair of President of the Senate, a motion was made, by one of his particular friends, in the senate, to confer TITLES on the officers of government, and to erect two or three RANKS or degrees of the members of the legislature. Let any person look into the minutes of the senate, then kept by Mr. Otis, (with the assistance of some of the senators, for he was not competent himself to that trifling task) and it will be discovered, that the senate was employed, for the greater part of two or three weeks, at the first organization of the government, on that *Illustrious* business, and which was so often rejected by the house of representatives, that they fairly shamed the senate out of it; and they,

instead of ordering the disgraceful transaction to be
erased from their books, with the tenacity of a child
to its hobby-horse, have entered on their minutes, in
words expressive of their sorrow, at not being able to
conform themselves to the customs of Europe, in regard to titles of Nobility; but that, from a desire of
keeping up a friendly intercourse with the house of
representatives, they would, *for the present*, postpone
the further consideration of the subject. Thus, they
have not entirely given up all hopes of reviving it at
some convenient moment hereafter; and thus this
bantling of Mr. Adams's brain was put out to nurse! I
wish they had torn the minutes of that debate from
their books, and sent them to Braintree with him on the
morning he ran away so early from Washington rather
than bear the sight of seeing Mr. Jefferson sworn into
office. I must not omit mentioning here, that it is
my opinion, had you at the time of the *illustrious*
debate, given it your hearty and sincere support, it
would have been carried through both houses of the
legislature, and we should now be disgusted with a
royal almanack published annually containing a

lengthy list of honorable Sedgwicks, right honourable
Thatchers, most honorable Ames', and *most illustrious*
Adamites. Your conduct on that occasion, therefore
deserves the highest approbation, whether it proceeded
from a luke-warmness to the scheme, or from a complete contempt of the effeminacy of so ridiculous a
project. Indeed, it would redound something further
to your credit, if you could yet prevail with some of
your friends in the present senate, to move for the
erasure of all the minutes that were foisted into the
books on that subject. And in doing this you would
only be acting in conformity with the opinions you
express in your letter to Mr. Adams so soon after the
dismissal of the army at Bristol. You, I am sure
gained no money or estates by your rank or pay, but
HE took care to feather his nest well for himself and
his young ones. So that he could the better bear your
attack. It would make a good caricature to sketch
him thus. Sitting snugly, in a warm nest, on the top
of a large weeping-willow at Braintree, looking down
at your headless body as it approaches from Fort-Pit,
which might be represented in the back ground all in

flames—Your head, as you said yourself, you would
never bring it back otherwise, might be exhibited as
following after you like a balloon in the air, whilst
Mr. Adams should appear in a full bag-wig with a
sort of glory around his head, and vast clouds in a
thousand fancied shapes and forms of coronets, scep-
tres, thrones, kingdoms, and millions of stars, and
garters. On his left breast a bulse of diamond with
the order of the WHITE DUCK in the centre. The trunk
of the willow should have scarlet-ribbond twining
like ivy in a spiral line with several gilt mottos such
as " *sola nobilitas virtus.*"   " *A deo et Rege.*"   " *Malum
mori quam fœderare,*" &c. And let a large OWL appear
high hovering in the air, in the act of *balancing a
straw.* Thus equipped and defended we leave him for
a moment to take a view of your mode of *bodily*
attack—with a full uniform, a truncheon in one hand,
and your LETTER in the other, you must appear in
the act of kicking your great jack-boots against the
root of the willow, until the Prussian Embassador,
who was placed there by way of cenitnel—seconds the
alarm, and calls out to his Pa, quack! quack! quack!

IT may offend some to see Mr. Adams thus satirised; but I submit to the world, whether his conduct in running away in the manner he did from Washington did not deserve the severest censure.—Did General Washington behave in this manner to him when he was first sworn into office at Philadelphia. No—he paid him all the respect possible and assumed no other consequence than that of a private citizen, and so did Mr. Jefferson, they both walked humbly in his train, Mr. Adams came down from the Senate chamber first, and I recollect that he, some how, neglected to foreshorten his sword whilst on the stairs, so that it trailed on the steps and made a noise that put me much in mind of the cat's feet to which a wicked boy had waxed walnut-shells, in order to frighten a family at midnight with suspicions of a ghost. I also recollect on the same occasion that when Mr. Adams entered the House of Representatives in order to be sworn, Mr. Jefferson was still Secretary of State, and had he been as ceremonious as the illustrious senators wanted to be, he would, as second officer in the government, have immediately followed the President, and Gen. Washington being sensible of the propriety thereof, and feeling himself only in the station of a private citizen, with that dignified simplicity and modesty that have ever characterized him, fell back on one side of the entrance, and bowing to Mr. Jefferson, whilst with his hand, he silently signified to him, to walk in before. But Mr. Jefferson, without a moment's hesitation, fell back also on the other side of the door; and after bowing to the general, he stood up firm and erect. It was the most interesting scene of elegant contention I had ever beheld, but lasted only about two seconds, and the general was obliged to enter first. I am the more particular in mentioning this circumstance, as it has been falsely propagated and published, that Mr. Jefferson was not an admirer of the general. I believe on the contrary he was the greatest bosom friend that the inspired Washington had in the world. Let his conduct on this occasion be compared to Mr. Adams's flight, and then answer me whether it had any of the symptoms of Nobility.

TOM CALLENDER.

LETTER IV.

SIR,

SINCE I have ventured to offer my humble assistance
in defence of the character of the virtuous Washington, against all detractors, it here occurs to my
memory, the villainous publication in London of an
Essay by that lowest of all rascals, Cobbett, in the
Anti-Jacobin Review, vol.5, page 547, which none of the
Aid-de-camps of our Commander in chief, have ever
yet taken the trouble to contradict—no, nor our di-
vines, who have been so busy in this city in defending
the fair fame of Col. Burr—nor the insolent Aber-
cromby at Philadelphia who was hand and glove with
that infernal enemy to all decency. I say, Sir, that it
appears to me on reflection, a little strange, that you
have never stepped forward to draw your pen in the
defence of your old commander. It is still more
strange that some of the clerical order have also omit-
ted to do it; and it is more than " passing strange,
'tis pitiful," that the author of Serious Considerations,
should find leisure sufficient from his holy studies, to

write a pamphlet of abusive language against Mr. Jefferson, who is a better christian than either himself or any of his coadjutors; and yet he could overlook the villainous slander of the British scoundrel, Cobbet. I appeal to all America, whether I can use any expression too harsh on such an occasion? I will now endeavour to wipe off the stain which that ruffian has attempted to cast upon the memory of a man, " the latchet of whose shoes he was not worthy to unloose."

The *aid* which was administered to Porcupine in New York and Philadelphia, *will* be an everlasting disgrace to the memories of those who supported *him*; whilst the glory of Washington will rise higher and higher in the estimation of every age hereafter.

In the book which I have alluded to, an attempt is made to give a review of American publications, and on the front of the list we find a single article containing a criticism on two distinct and separate subjects; the one of which is the eulogium delivered by a gentleman of the American revolutionary army on the character of Gen. Washington.—The other, a prayer of a clergyman at the opening of an innocent

ceremony of respect to departed virtue, which happened shortly after the account of that great man's
death had reached that city.

The anti-jacobin *reviewer*, whose abilities compared
to those of the old reviewers is like charcoal to dia-
monds, commences his criticism with a few lines of
pirated language, and afterwards falls into his own
low and pitiful abuse. The first paragraph is—" If
every individual were an insulated being, who lived
for himself, agreeably to the new system of certain
German philosophists, no detriment to society could
accrue from a rigid adherence to the ancient maxim
—*De mortuis nil nisi bonum.* But so long as salutory
lessons of a religious and political nature are to be
deduced—so long as moral inclinations for the use
and benefit of society are to be derived from the
conduct and characters of men, who have made a
conspicuous figure on the theatre of life—so long
shall we continue to reprehend a strict observance
of such a maxim, as calculated to deprive mankind
of the advantages of *example*, which interest alike
the heart and the understanding, and eminently con-

tribute to promote the cause of virtue. The *nil nisi verum* is the only rule worthy of attention, in the delineation of public characters."

To this paragraph an easy answer occurs.—True, it will offend not only many and excellent men, but it must offend every excellent man to know that any attempt to diminish the respect that is justly due to the memory of Washington, especially when it is considered that the attempt has been made by such a vile miscreant. " Accustomed to make sacrifices to truth," as he says of himself, but which all good men will instantly understand the true meaning to be, *accustomed to sacrifice all truth and decency*; and as to his not yielding to the tide of popular prejudice—every sensible man knows, that a long series of popular opinion amounts as nearly to truth as any theorem in fluxions. Sir Isaac Newton would not, were he living, deny it, although this cobweb-brusher of a book-store has the spitefulness to oppose it.

THE Americans have not been too lavish of their commendations on their hero—for the effusion of a few individuals, who may have over-stept the bounds

of mechanic language, yet had, nevertheless, a good
intention in every word they spoke; and although they
may have committed some little mistakes, in the
modus in rebus, still their hearts, at the time they were
speaking, were *fortiter in re*—this is only borrowing
the words of one of the greatest English politicians.

In the first instance, we find that the philanthropy
and philosophy of ancient maxims are rejected, to
make way for the *nil nisi verum*, " in order to promote
the cause of virtue!"—and, in the same piece, the
writer, afterwards, condemns the episcopal clergy, for
having deviated from the *old established* orthodox rules
and orders of the ages of ignorance and superstition.
He pretends to a knowledge of the affairs of the
churches; we shall see presently how well informed
he is on that subject:

" The advantages of *example* which equally interest
the heart and the understanding," he says, are refused
to him, if he were obliged to pay respect to the old
maxim, *de mortuis nil nisi bonum*; ergo, he leaps over
all the bounds of both ancient and modern decency
and truth, and, under a mask of searching after ve-

racity, he, unequivocally, attempts to hold up the character of one of the TRUEST Men that ever lived, as an example—for what;—not for imitation! but quite the contrary! I am ashamed to follow up this rascally insinuation any further, nor would I have ever condescended to bring this impotent magazine into view, were it not I know many individuals in America who take a secret malicious pleasure in supporting *some* foreigners, who ultimately prove to be their deeprooted enemies.

IF the despicable author of the Review means to insinuate, whieh I am sure he does, that general Washington has *not* contributed to the cause of virtue—then all the good and great men on the face of this globe, who have admired and praised the virtue of our Patriot Chief, must be very ignorant, indeed, or this disgraceful British Reviewer must be so abominable a ———, that Milton's description of Satan would not afford colours sufficiently black to paint him in.

THERE shall be millions of millions hereafter, of the BEST and BRAVEST of mankind, to speak and write in the most ardent praise of WASHINGTON.

7

His second paragraph goes thus: " A church is, as-
suredly, the most improper of all places for the de-
livery of a professed *eulogium*. The temple of Truth
should never be polluted by the strains of adulation.
And flattery more gross, seldom, we conceive, escaped
the lips of man, in any place whatever. ' Who shall
delineate a just portrait of that character which was
perfect in all its relations—or in what language shall
the story of that life be told, where every action was
above all praise?' Again—' the god-like Washington'
—' this immaculate man.' This language is really
impious, and what kind of credit can be given to the
facts stated by a man who so far forgets himself as to
use it? Our objections, however, are principally con-
fined to the use of these unjustifiable terms. The
orator has not imitated some of *his* countrymen, who,
on a similar occasion, dared to stigmatize *this* country
and its sovereign; his other sins are not so much sins
of commission as sins of ' *omission;*' he has only
shewn one side, and that the fair side of the picture;
though indeed, by calling his hero *immaculate*, he denies that there were any spots in his character. Pre-

sumptious and foolish man, to hold up a '*a monster
of perfection*' to the world, and to call on its inhabitants to admire and worship it!"

Thus far has this impertinent reviewer attempted
in his second paragraph, and thus we reply:

In every country, a church is the most proper place
for delivering a funeral discourse. I appeal to all the
world, if this reviewer doth not here express a self-evi-
proof of malice propense? buoyed up, as he was, by
a vain expectation of support from a party (heaven
be praised, there is no party now existing in any
country or climate who does not renounce and despise
him) of earning bread by the most dishonourable of
all meannesses—the sales of scandal—he still ventures
farther, and with diabolical effrontery, insinuates, that
the temple of Truth had been polluted by the strains
of adulation and flattery; and boldly asks, what kind
of credit is to be given to the orator who delivered
the eulogium?

This is indirectly telling the gentleman that he
spoke falsehoods within the walls of the temple of
Truth; for, all the little attempts that follow *that*

assertion, by way of qualifying it, will never alter the
express meaning of the writer. If he had not been
at the distance of more than three thousand miles
from the orator, it is highly probable that gentleman
would have obliged him to modify the words, by
argumentum ad rem; at least, I believe so, in case he
would descend to notice the calumniator.

But, this creature shews, in almost every instance,
a complete ignorance of men and things in America:
for here he says, "The orator has not imitated some
of *his* countrymen, who dared to stigmatize this
country (England) and its sovereign." Here an absolute lie is broached. If he means that the orator
was an American, he is entirely wrong : that gentleman was a native of Great Britain, and, it is presumed,
had no occasion to be propped up by the faint
apologies of any foreign emissary, for such is the
meaning of the passage, " his other sins are not so
much the sins of commission as sins of omission."

As to the bullying words, "dared to stigmatize this
country and its sovereign," such language might have
passed in the camp at Saratoga, before the capitula-

tion of the brilliant *nil nisi bonum* general; but, at this day, a threat like this, can only serve to excite risibilty in every man's countenance, whose muscles have not lost the power of smiling.

THE orator held up the fair side of the picture, because there was no foul side to be shewn. Yet, an infamous scavenger of literature shall attempt to twist this picture into a monster of perfection.

The third division of the reviewer's iniquitous publication is as follows:—"We are well aware that, by attempting to diminish the respect which has been so lavishly bestowed on the memory of Washington, we shall give serious offence to many excellent and worthy men. But, we are accustomed to make sacrifices to *truth*, and we do not feel disposed in the present instance, to yield to the tide of popular prejudice, and shrink from the discharge of a public duty. Let the Americans, if they think proper, lavish their commendations on their hero, for establishing their blessed republic—with that we have nothing to do; but, for ourselves, feeling as Englishmen, and as loyal subjects, *we* never can contemplate the public charac-

ter of Washington, without seeing, as its prominent
feature, the horrid crime of rebellion, which nothing
but *repentance* can ever efface. It is not success which
diminishes the guilt of a criminal. To America, then,
Washington might be a *hero;* to Britain he was a
TRAITOR. Nor is this the only protest we have to
enter against the *spotless purity* of this 'immaculate,'
this 'God-like' man. If we have not been very
much misinformed, general WASHINGTON was a *deist.*
We have not forgotten his reception of the flag sent
him by ROBESPIERRE, nor his declaration, at the
same time, that he '*approved* of the French revolution in its *commencement,* its *progress* and its *result.*'
As to his disinterestedness, of which so much has been
said, formerly by Thomas Paine, and lately by other
sycophants in America; who have carried their impudence so far as to assert that he never even accepted
a *salary;* we have it in our power to accuse those
gentlemen of advancing willful falsehoods. General
Washington not only took care to receive his salary
regularly, (for which certainly no blame could attach
to him) but even touched a great portion of the

salary of the ensuing year, by which means he had an
opportunity of speculating with the public money.
This fact, we know, was the subject of public contro-
versy in America, and the proofs of its existence,
were never invalidated!'

"Angels and ministers of grace defend us"—from
such a bare-faced villain as this—He calls Washington a DEIST, and a SPECULATOR with the public money?—Where! O where! wert thou then, Camillus,
Phocius, Publius, General, Royal-Fed?—Where wert
thou Serious Consideration—Trumpeter—Voice of
Warning?—All asleep. Washington was in the cold
tomb—had he been living, your ten thousand pens
would have leapt out of ten thousand wings in his defence—but he was dead, and you could no longer
expect promotions from him.—Ye all began to worship
the rising-sun, John Adams, of whom you expected to
make a very tool for your own purposes.

THE honor and pleasure of confuting the villain,
devolves to me, and I wrote something similar to this,
which I sent to London nearly two years ago, where
it had some effect in raising up the resentment of

the citizens at the time Cobbet's house was demolished.

I now assert—that Washington was a pure christian, and it is well known to every person who ever knew him, that he was a liberal respecter of every religion, without being a persecutor. I next affirm that he never speculated with the public money to the amount of a single cent, or a thousand, or a million of cents, dollars or pounds. I lastly declare that the charge made by the British brute, of his having touched his salary in advance, is as abominable a lie, as if any wretch were to assert that there is no God. The only foundation which Cobbett had for the malicious falsehood, proceeded from a very ill-judged paragraph in the Aurora, whilst that paper was conducted by B. F. Bache, who was unfortunately influenced by his father, who had a private pique against Washington, to publish it. Every one knows that there is a law existing which allows the President of the United States to receive a salary of twenty-five thousand dollars per annum. The President's private secretary was in the habit of taking up this salary, either

monthly ·or quarterly, and he was regular in the
duties of his office. It happened however that there
was a trifling informality in the report of the Secretary of the treasury, Wolcott, who ought to particu-
larize the items of the appropriations for the year.—
He conceived that the law for paying the President's
salary was sufficient, and he forgot to mention it in
his report to the committee of ways and means.—
Thus, although the law existed for paying the President's salary, there was not any specific appropriation.
Some imp of ˙darkness communicated this to old
Bache, who influenced his son, the proprietor of the
Aurora, to give it publicity, and to make it appear
that Gen. Washington was receiving pay in advance.
The British villain inconsiderately grabbed at the
mistake, and has dared to publish it to the world in
the above paragraph in the Anti-Jacobin Review.

THE truth must now clearly appear to every man
of common intellect, that neither Gen. Washington,
nor his secretary, knew any thing about Wolcott's
blunder; the secretary went on in his usual mode—
the law was his authority—but with regard to the

8

taking up a single sixpence in advance—there can be no greater falsehood uttered. Gen. Washington was never in want of money for himself, neither did he ever take up any from the public coffers but for the best and noblest purposes. To follow the slanderer any farther, would 'be superfluous—and I really believe, that although our sanctified gentlemen in America suffered Cobbet to print that anti-jacobin review, and subscribed for it, the citizens of London, when they see this statement, will not hesitate to pull down the fellow's house again about his ears.

But, it is too much the practice with partial politicians to read those kind of scurrilous pamphlets.—They sell the better for being detestable, and so it was with Wood, Callender, Philænus, and all the rest of the gang of detractors, who have played into each other's hands too long, to the great disgrace of the printing art, as well as the annoyance of the public. To follow Cobbet through the whole of the review, would be too tedious for some of our readers; I will, therefore, select such paragraphs as seem to be particularly levelled at the character and memory of general WASHINGTON. His seventh phillippic proceeds thus:

"Whilst the congress was employed in passing their mournful resolutions, and their funeral admonitions to the pious inhabitants of the United States, they were laughing in their sleeves at the dupes which they had made, and the impositions which they had passed on the world. The fact is, that, notwithstanding the dissentions which prevail among the contending parties of enlightened statesmen, in *one wish* they are *unanimous*—to DECEIVE foreigners and foreign nations. But the attempt is as fruitless as the wish is dishonourable. In this general mourning, prescribed by patriotic hypocrisy, and enforced by popular authority, it is not an uncommon thing to see members with crape on their arms, and, at the same time, to hear them vent maledictions on the memory of the deceased!——One other fact, on the authenticity of which they may fully rely, will suffice to shew our readers what sort of freedom of thought and action the Americans are allowed to enjoy, and what sincerity of soul is concealed under the outer trappings of woe. A gentleman having been asked why he did not wear crape on his arm, answered, that, he thanked God, he had lost neither relation nor friend. 'What!' exclaimed the querist, 'was not general Washington your friend?' 'No,' rejoined the other, 'he was no man's friend; and it would have been a good thing had he died twenty years ago.' This blunt declaration was immediately succeeded by a threat of vengeance from the querist; and it was with great difficulty that the gentleman escaped the yankee punishment of *tar and feather*, and that his house was rescued from destruction, by his consent to *wear* a crape, and to ask pardon standing publickly on a table! In relating this fact, we must not be supposed to acquiesce in the unqualified assertion, that general Washington was the friend of no man; we are not sufficiently acquainted with the general's private character to vouch for the validity of so serious a charge; and we are extremely unwilling to believe, that a man who has been so highly and so warmly praised, in different countries, though we know how to appreciate such praise, could really

deserve an accusation, which implies a disposition we
should shudder to contemplate."

The circumstance, or something similar did take
place in New-York; but the gentleman alluded to, in
my opinion, ought not to be much obliged to the reviewer, for trumping it up to the world again, after it
had been nearly buried in oblivion. I will not, therefore, take any further notice of it, to hurt the feelings
of a person for whom I have a high respect, only to
make a remark on the reviewer's malicious con-
clusions.

In the beginning of the foregoing paragraph, he
endeavours to cast a general stain upon all America—
he ridicules both our civil and religious societies, and
condemns our laws almost in toto. Whatever respect
he may be thought entitled to from the gentlemen of
the bar, on these points, they are best able to judge
of themselves. One thing must be allowed to them,
and, I believe, much to their honor—that they have
found laws sufficient to punish emissaries and slan-
derers, who may have been employed by foreign nations for bad purposes amongst us; and in some cases

they have obliged the miscreants to fly from our shores.

As to the attack upon our religious orders, it appears strange that some of them have hitherto neglected to reply to the calumnies of this same foreign reviewer. It will be but a poor reason in them to alledge, that "he is such a scoundrel, he is not worth their notice—neither himself nor his writings."

AND, is this all ye will say, ye reverend friends and daily associates of your once favorite and delightful Peter Porcupine! Why, I could make a much better excuse for you myself; but I will not at present draw up the curtain, behind which you have, in so cowardly a manner, hid your plotting heads. It is only to you, the *Skulkers*, I allude; and, God be praised, ye are but a small number, compared with the thousands of open, undesigning, honest men, of every church.

THE elegant comparison of "*mild and stale*," when speaking of the proceedings of the episcopal clergy at their convention, held some time ago, at Philadel-

phia, is amougst the number of the *compliments* paid
to them, and is thus as elegantly compared to retailers
of porter mixing *mild* with *stale* beer;—and, lastly,
this mixture of the CLERGY with the LAITY, is said to
be like "plowing with the *Ox* and the *Ass* together."
See here, reverend gentlemen, how this old acquaintance of some of ye, makes *Oxen* of you and *Asses* of
the laity! And have you tamely submitted to all
this scurrillity? If your compatriot was here (I
mean the compatriots of half a dozen, or a few more,
clergymen, whom I know well; but, from pure charity,
will here omit personifying), it is highly probable
that ye would expose one another, as has been the
case lately between men of much higher notoriety in
this country, who have commenced a clumsy and
awkward war against each other. Adieu, ye reverend
few; cover your faces with your gowns, lest the true
and faithful christians should be further provoked to
shew the hypocrisy of your hearts.

AFTER having taken the foregoing view of the
slanders propagated by this *British enemy*, (for he is
more *their* enemy than he has in his power to be *ours*)

it is time to *finish* him with some general observations.

WITH his private or personal character, whether as a soldier, a spy, an impostor, or an incendiary, I have nothing to do; although he has, during his short residence in America, been encouraged by some friendly people to invade and abuse the most sacred and domestic concerns of churches, houses, camps, country, male, female, old, and young, without mercy or distinction. Shame on those who supported him; but, some of them have been since laid low. For the living, as well as the dead, a respect towards their children's future prosperity, forbids my enumerating their names, although I know them as well as I know the little corrosive sublimate of PARSONS, who will hereafter be despised by their brethren; and, indeed, in Philadelphia they are all known, and their views as clearly intelligible to Americans, as the writing on the wall was understood by Belteshazzar's interpreter.

THE whole drift of the performance in question, it is evident, as I have already said, is, to vent the spleen of an individual, who values himself on the

honor of having been born in England, but whose
conduct has been a disgrace to the name of a Briton!
Who is the Briton that dare shew his face in any
company of honourable men, in any country, and
utter the words which this itinerant vagabond has
found means to get published? Shame on the beg-
garly printer's poverty of soul, who would prostitute
his types to such a vile purpose. He must be very
poor, indeed—starving for bread—to sell such poison
to procure it;—better he had been sent to Botany-
Bay, there to live upon the mandrake-plant, than
basely thus to procure a sustenance in London, by is-
suing forth such villainous falsehoods, that there is
not a child of six years old from Japan to California,
or from Baffin's Bay to New Zealand, but would say,
" you have deceived us, and we cannot but despise
you."

But, in order to fill up the measure of his iniquity,
he contradicts the very accounts published all over
the world, descriptive of the most sincere and profound sorrow which was every where expressed on
this truly melancholy occasion, and in those holy

9

sanctorums wherever the funeral eulogiums were delivered; nay, he denies that the people shed tears:
These are his words—

"Now, we have good authority for saying, that, in
Philadelphia, where this prayer was delivered, not a
wet eye was to be seen on the occasion. The three
hymns at the conclusion of the prayer, are miserable
imitations of Sternhold and Hopkins."

IN answer to this, I need only refer to yourself, Mr.
Hamilton, who I saw, on that day, shedding tears. I
must also refer to Mr. Jefferson, who, likewise, shed
tears plentifully, as did hundreds of other gentlemen
and ladies who were present, and thousands of spec-
tators who crowded the streets to see the procession.

BUT, the reviewer follows the immortal Hero of our
Country even into the silent tomb, with all the studied
rancour, falsehood, and treachery of an imp of hell.
And yet, it is reported, that there are several hundred
subscribers to that book in this country. In America!
forbid it, Patriotism—forbid it, Gratitude—forbid it,
Virtue. Oh, Death, where is thy sting?—O, Grave,
where is thy victory?——That those subscribers may

reflect more wisely, and withdraw their support from this foreign reviler of our country, ourselves, and our laws, ought to be the sincere wish of every good and virtuous citizen.

Tom Callender.

LETTER V.

Sir,

Having, in my last letter, I presume, wiped off all the stains that the British critic had attempted to cast upon the character of general Washington, I shall next perform the same office of respect to the character of Mr. Jefferson, which has been as wickedly attacked here by another Porcupine, under the modest signature of Junius Philænus, and, as I apprehend, Sir, under your patronage. It will, also, be a part of my task, to say something in defence of old governor Clinton, and some other gentlemen who have been so basely traduced in your favorite News-papers.—The affectionate esteem which general Washington always expressed towards governor Clinton, is well known to

the world—and even in his last will, the name of that
gentleman is mentioned in a particularly respectful
manner. This is sufficient to give the lie direct to
any of your scribblers, who have said that governor
Clinton was inimical to the general—and, I am certain, I may solemnly assert the same in regard to the
friendship which exists between Mr. Jefferson and the
governor.

THEY have always been true friends, nor can any
deep-laid plot or schism divide them. The pamphlet-
eers and paragraph writers cannot be considered, by
men of sense and probity, as of the least consequence.
The farmers of North America must know that they
are now more happy, comfortable and secure, than
they were under the last administration, because they
have not to pay ten dollars per year, or some such tax,
for riding out in their own chair.—No window-tax,
which was contemplated, will vex their feelings—
stamps will not interrupt the negociations between
man and man—excises are gone to the dogs—&c. &c.
These are arguments so strong that the most red-hot Fed,
will scarcely have effrontory sufficient to deny them;

neither will the pilot-boat speculator, or any of the *imported citizens* of America, after the war was over, " and nothing in our mind but joy." That man was no citizen of the United States, although he was permitted to take a seat in congress, and afterwards to partake of the most honorable and lucrative offices. He benefited himself by his knowledge of what was going on, and what was expected to end in favor of the intricate British system of finance, set up by you, *a la mode de monsieur Pitt*, but which has turned out to be not so bad as you intended it—an *ever lasting* burthen —a mill-stone hung around the necks of the people to bring them into subjection, and, then, in case that plan failed, you were to have a standing army to reduce them into obedience—Bravo! Surely it was then a good time to wrest the power from such hands.— It would be needless to say any more of that deep and deadly policy. The present administratien have, with a masterly hand, retrieved us out of those desperate dilemmas into which we were likely to be sunk forever.—Your policy was not only wrong in theory, but has been worse in practice; allowing your heart to have had no share in it. Reduced as you are to such a situation as this—when your friends as well as your adversaries in politics (for I cannot suppose you have any personal enemies) have all agreed upon one conclusion, that you are a mistaken politician, with all your great and undeniable abilities. Then, when you find this to be the case, why not permit us to enjoy the benefits of our present mild (though nationally honorable and firm) administration? why not allow us to give to it the same chance of experiment that you required for *yours?* THE PEOPLE are satisfied with the present administration, would you and your satellites permit us to be happy and comfortable.

COLEMAN, whom I know not whether he is a white or black-*man*, is not only supposed to be your principal typographer, but it has been clearly ascertained. Gracious Heavens! How can *you* as a man, patronize such a fellow? whose trade is scandal, whose bread depends upon the circulation of falsehood? his miscariages of criticism upon every thing he has attempted are a disgrace to literature. Even on the subject of the theatre, he, *your* Coleman, and an apothecary,

" whom I remember that hereabouts doth dwell, cull-
ing of simples, and old cakes of roses."

THEY have the assurance to issue forth THEIR criticisms on theatricals. I think it necessary to bring in
this subject to shew, that it is a *junto* of the *same degree*
of the knights of the gray-goose-wing that write
against the president, the people, and the theatre. I
am therefore, justified in bringing in this remark.—
Two or three Scriblerusses, I really believe, have got
the freedom of the house (theatre) from the manager,
and they are obliged to repay him in the humble coin
of publishing whatever he dictates. Thus all the performers lie at the mercy of the manager, whose only
merit lies in the translation of a few stupid German
plays of which it would take more than *five-hundred*
to make *one* plot like Shakespeare's Hamlet.

THE impudence of these critics, must appear evident to every man of taste who has seen the world.—
Those "minor critics" have had the assurance to bla-
zon forth the merits of subaltern performers, and then
throw cold water upon the first-rate. They have
evinced this disposition in their *multum in parvo*

remarks upon Mr. Hodgkinson, to whom they will allow no other merit, than, that " he performed his part with propriety." Here is a silent intention of black and vindictive malice, let it come from what quarter it may. And to which I reply, that Hodgkinson is the best general performer I have known. In the same strain of hireling criticism—those Irvings, and Colemans, and the poor apothecaries and their apprentices have been itching to attack Mrs. Whitlock, whose powers cannot be found out by any of this band of critics. Yet every person of genuine taste must admit that she is the best performer that has yet appeared in America. Let those demi-critics dare to say that they have ever seen such acting as her's in *Estiphania?* yet they freeze at the thought of paying her the smallest compliment. They undoubtedly are authorized in thus manœuvering by the manager, whose time would be better employed in ordering the regulation of the under characters of every play.—Garrick would not permit a messenger to deliver a message to himself unless the performer *understood* the subject and looked him full in the face.—But, Mr. Dunlap, thinks all this under-management unnecessary—if so, how can the first performers exert their talents? how could Hodgkinson, in Dionisius, harrangue his soldiers when *they* stood like a row of pallisadoes at the back of the stage, and if he had addressed them in that position, he must have turned his back upon the audience.—There was no body to tell them what to do, but Hodgkinson himself, and I heard him whisper something to the TROOPS, after which they *marched* in *detour* so as to form a front on the side scenes. I mention these things to shew the influence of the managers on those writers of criticisms, and also to intimate the power of Mr. Hamilton over the writers for Coleman, Bayard and Lang.

COLEMAN in humble imitation of the rest of these bribed critics of Mr. Dunlap, must also come on, limping after these, with his sagacious and most perspicuous remarks; but, if he does not cut a better figure in that field of fancy than he has on the political theatre, he had better beat a retreat quickly to the tune of "The General,"—"Strike your tent and march away."

10

THE abusive language which this man has intro-
duced into the Evening Post is more base and vile
than that of Porcupine or Callender—it is even equal
to Lang's insolent publication of L***'s most malig-
nant gall, or the Commercial Editor's attempts at
writing.

BUT I can account for this last mentioned gentleman's insolence. He was intended for a lawyer by
Papa who was a vendue master in Philadelphia; but
some how, he was not the kind of wood to make a
Mercury of; therefore he did not succeed at the bar.
His friends, however, made interest to get him appointed Clerk of the Circuit Court of Pennsylvania,
at the first meeting of that Court in Philadelphia,
when Mr. Jay was Chief Justice of the United States,
and appeared on the bench in party-colored silken
robes, as flashy as any Roman Bishop ever wore when
performing the ceremony of high mass on an Easter
holiday. The post of Clerk was not lucrative enough
to make a permanent living for our Editor—there was
scarcely any business to be transacted in the court at
that time, as there was no *Alien* or *Sedition* laws exist-

ing under Washington's administration.—Those disgraceful acts were left for his successor to manufacture.

The post therefore conferred on our Editor was no more than a feather in his cap, which would never support a family, and as he was now entered on the list of office-hunters, he made application for another post, which, through the interest of his connections, he obtained.—He was appointed to go to London to assist in settling the disputed claims of the Americans with the English merchants for marine spoliations; towards which he contributed very little.— The credit of that settlement is due to our Ambassador, Rufus King, who very judiciously finished the work by a single dash of his pen, by boldly lumping the whole intricacy of the various claims into one consolidated sum, which is so well known to the public as to render it unnecessary to say anything further on the subject, at present; only to remark, that our Editor's office was consequently rendered null and void; and, as he could not live in London upon the air, without a salary, he very prudently returned to his native soil, very much chagrined against our administration, for not continuing him in pay after the office was abolished.

This accounts in one measure for his resentment against Mr. Jefferson ever since. There is another reason which also, probably operates on his gall—The repeal of the judiciary *extravaganza*, whereby Judge Baffet lost his birth, who is father-in-law to a near relation of our editor, and who has also lost his election in Deleware, by the consent of the *voce populi*.

These are facts, to which our editor has not sufficient philosophy to submit, although they are the common result of natural causes. He therefore, has set up a barking and yelping in conjunction with the rest of the whole pack of hounds that have been striving to hunt down the fair fame of our first magistrate; and what makes it still the more disgustful is, the patronage given to this pack by you, Sir, whose station in life ought to prevent your sinking into such pitiful arts, and scandalous libels. It is from these provocations that I have thought you, Sir, (Mr. Hamilton) the most proper personage to address these letters to; and because I despise your emissaries too much, to descend into a correspondence with *them*, whilst you are so prominent in my view.

The pilot-boat expedition of *Smith, Duer, and Co.* are still well recollected. Whilst your funding system was on the carpet; and when a right calculation could be formed on the vote that would be carried for it in preference to Mr. Madison's propositions—whilst it was yet pending, those speculating companies took up all the hard money they could borrow on their credit, &c. and sent it off by a troop of brokers and clerks, in pilot-boats and stages, who were dispersed through Carolina, and some other states to purchase up the poor soldier's certificates at two shillings and six-pence for the pound, and perhaps for less than that poor *equivalent.* Those gentlemen knew their game, and although you had no hand in that job, you certainly winked at it. Another plot of a deeper dye was likewise attempted on the members of the United States legislature, when an effort was made to purchase the votes of some of them, to vote for a law to grant a charter to a company of land-jobbers for the dominion of a large tract of country, whereby they would all of them become a train of petty princes. Their mode of address was to issue certain vouchers or tickets, like lottery-tickets—payable only *to bearer*; so that even should those tickets be found in possession of any of them, no name being inserted, the bribed member could not be discovered.—This plot failed—there were a sufficient number in congress resist, and reject the base attempt, as there ever will be.—The aggregate wisdom and virtue of our general legislature, will always oppose such attempts.

I will here take the liberty of recording some others of the same stamp. The bank of North America, was set up with the king of France's dollars, sent here to pay the revolutionary army, when they were on the point of a mutiny—yet Mr. Robt. Morris, with the assistance of his advisers, had the address to *satisfy* the soldiers with his own six months notes without ever allowing the honest fellows to palm a six-pence of the cash. The money was made into a bank, and the soldiers were paid with notes, with which they purchased shoes at ten dollars the pair, hats, &c. on the same *reasonable* terms, at various stores, set up by this Robert Morris, and his agents, in every quarter of the United States; so that in the end the soldiers never touched the money, although he made the profit.

But see what is the consequence of ill-gotten wealth —it is like an East India fortune, never goes to a third generation. This same Mr. financier-general of the United States, who acted this character towards the people, and who also played some *l'argent* tricks upon the Marquis la Fayette—he—the mighty man has *fallen,* as many, many more of your acquaintance have done—Greenleaf—Nicholson, &c.—The Eastern and Southern cognoscenti in speculation—yet these are the sort of men that want to recover the reins of our government—these are the men who come in flocks to consult with you in New-York upon a plan or plot of operation against the present safe and mild administration. Let them beware how far they proceed—let them pause, with *Monsieur le Governeur,* as Porcupine calls him—let your tribes of calumniating editors with all their thousand tongues—let your secret-working hypocritical parsons—your out-of-office fallen angels—let even the Jersey Jove, and *you*, Sir, beware how far you carry on this trade of iniquity, lest the people should be roused with indignation against your Satanic incantations and despotic systems, and in their honest zeal pronounce them TREASON!

TOM CALLENDER.

LETTER VI.

SIR,

I HAVE always considered it to be an indispensible duty of the editors of news-papers to render to the public who support them, a due account of such information as may have fallen within the sphere of their knowledge, especially of circumstances relative to the wellfare or danger of the state. Amongst the multiplicity of objects that are daily bursting on their view, and whilst so much notice has been taken of our domestic pamphlets, it seems strange that these editors should overlook or neglect noticing, or answering, the infamous slanders of both foreign and domestic intruders upon all decency and civil government; some of whom have been nursed in the bosom of America, and others fostered amongst us, who only waited for an opportunity to sting the hand that raised them from obscurity into situations of profit and honor. Even two or three of our doctors of divinity have incurred the detestation of their own congregations, who have informed me of this fact, and who were accustomed to attend their discourses with pure delight; but who have since deserted them, in consequence of their having deserted their duty to God, by becoming the mean instruments of polemical intrigue or dark and dismal tyranny, which was tried and weighed in the scales of unsuccessful ambition. The mercantile interest of this country to whom I wish to pay a real respect, will now confess how much they were mistaken by patronizing (some of them) Porcupine's Gazette, the editor of which (Cobbet) since his return to England has thrown off the mask of Federalism, and now exhibits himself in native

11

colours—that he was only a spy whilst he was here, that he wishes to injure and destroy the mutual intercourse and commerce between that nation and this, which it is our interest, as well as theirs, to preserve most inviolably. He endeavors to throw us into contempt in the eyes of the British merchants—to injure and wound for ever, if he could, the credit and character of America.

· My friends—ye merchants of the United States— tell me, is this not the fact ?—When you read his review you must acknowledge it, and you must all be of one opinion, that he has betrayed you in such a style as to force from you an ejaculation—" he is the blackest of traitors."—For the honor of humanity, nevertheless, I cannot suppose that the honest and enlightened merchants of either England or America, or of any other country under Heaven, would be influenced by the falsehoods and scurrility of the veriest ruffian that ever disgraced the freedom of the press. Under this impression, I would be inclined to think that his attacks upon America and the citizens of the United States, although published in London in a daily newspaper, will not have any injurious effect to the well-established trade between the two countries. The treacherous attempts of a few despicable Englishmen, to prevent our having a good breed of sheep, by purchasing and killing them, to send away as salted provisions—to burn a spinning machine at Philadelphia, lest we should go on with the cotton or any other manufactory—all these things I despise, nor do I put it to the charge or account against the British nation. If there be any truth in the whole of these charges, the shame ought to rest upon the individuals who perpetrated the crime, for I solemnly declare that no man could make me believe that the government, or the people of that country, would or could ever countenance such an abominable proceeding. The British are too enlightened a nation to suffer a stigma like this upon their character. There may be some envious persons whose speculations into futurity will not carry them farther than the length of their noses; but there are thousands of Englishmen who contemplate America in a very different point of view, and who can clearly perceive the rising consequence

of the United States, and our rapid career towards a
station of more sublime consequence than any of the
antient or modern nations could ever boast of.—Nor
is the time so very distant when this great æra will
take place.   Less than half a century will verify this
prediction, and exhibit to the world an American navy
equal to that of any other nation that may THEN be in
existence, notwithstanding the insiduous plots and
schemes of either internal or external foes to cramp
or confuse us.   I will also hazard another assertion
still stronger than the last.   That, THE UNITED STATES
OF AMERICA WILL CONTINUE TO BE A REPUBLIC.   The idle
conjectures of all the politicians in the world cannot
prevent it.   The visionary hopes of Mr. Adams cannot
prevent it, nor all the powers of Europe in conjunction.   This may appear to some persons to be too extravagant an idea—but I think it is a conclusion that
may be fairly deduced from sound doctrine and just
calculation.—FRANCE!   AMERICANS set the example, in
their revolt from tyranny, for you to imitate ; but
it has been reserved for FRENCHMEN to decide the most
important question that has ever been agitated in the

world! The annals of this earth afford no similar instance of a period so highly interesting to humanity. The great and glorious problem has been solved—whether mankind were born to be the everlasting dupes and slaves of ten or a dozen murdering despots; or whether the God of Nature created this globe for the use of its inhabitants? The decision has been in favor of the people—the dispute was between men and kings: France and America have both succeeded, and although there may at present be vested too high a degree of arbitrary power in the hand of the chief magistrate, I have the strong hope and assurance in my own mind that the Republican form of government will nevertheless be preserved there as well as in this country.—France alone by the real equality of its individuals as to knowledge and manners is most capable of perfect freedom; but it has become fashionable among a certain class of men, to depreciate the very principles of liberty and equality of election; because, some temporary effects have taken place in France, from the confusion of the times, that will not bear a vindication. Let those gentlemen, however, consider and enquire, " whether these effects, as far as they are unfortunate, are not derived from the treachery of those who expended the revenue allowed them by the NEW system, in endeavoring to restore the OLD one ?" And if these effects are found to have been so procured, what should result from the discovery but a confirmed abhorrence of the OLD system and of that political creed, which invites men to crimes by rendering THEM sacred."

THE same argument will apply to this country under the last administration, as it does likewise to your ideas of forms of government which you had the boldness to propose in the convention of 1787. The plan you proposed was happily rejected, and the constitution which was adopted has been so wisely and prudently amended, that it now gives complete security to THE PEOPLE in general, and I am sure it will be carried on with satisfaction by the present administration, in despite of all the important attacks of yourself and the weak opposition of your coadjutors, who will not allow that all mankind are competent to judge of the best form of government for their general happiness—

your doctrine is, that a few kingly animals are more competent, who have been and ever will be (so long as the earth is burthened with them) educated by servile flatterers, impostors, and slaves. It is a melancholy truth, that in this enlightened age, there should still be found, even in America, men who will advocate an hereditary chief magistracy. "The experience of past ages," say they, "justifies us in this conclusion —that although republican forms of government are the most natural and approved systems, yet the inclination of parties seem to bend so quickly toward monarchy, we had better come to it at once, in order to prevent troublesome altercations and political disquisitions." Thus—would these FRIENDS of republicanism surrender the divine and natural rights of man, rather than struggle against the artful encroachments of false and ungodly doctrine. But the present government of the United States is republican and will remain so, I hope, for ever—and will always furnish a sufficient confutation of this mistaken axiom; and always put a stop to the ambitious views of men who wanted to cry "havoc" and let loose "the dogs of war!"

THIS hankering after a standing army, must proceed from some evil spirit that hath taken possession of some of our citizens, and ought to be kept under— accordingly we have set it down for a thousand years, as is mentioned in the book of the revelations of St. John, chapter xx. " And I saw an angel come down from Heaven, having the key of the bottomless pit, and a great *chain* in his hand.—And he laid hold on the dragon, (War,) that old serpent, which is the Devil, and Satan, and bound him a thousand years— And cast him into the bottomless pit, and shut him up, and set a seal upon him, that he should deceive the nations no more, till the thousand years should be fulfilled," &c.

HAVING thus got rid of you and your intrigues, as it is " devoutly to be wished," for a thousand years, we expect that our government and administration will go on with the same degree of characteristical firmness, and prudence that it commenced with.—The yells of Discontents will be set down to the account of their own folly.—With regard to myself, I never held any place or pension under the government; nor do I believe I ever shall ; nor do I expect to receive any more emolument for publishing these letters than you did when you made a present (to Mr. Lang) of the Copyright of your letter addressed to poor John Adams. I am as independent as you are in mind and body. The individual or collective interest of the Clintonians, Hamiltonians, or Jeffersonians, could never operate on my mind so long as a single second of time.—Our government is now safe, and the administration of it secure ; nor shall any of our internal, or external enemies dare to overturn it.

Tom Callender.

F I N I S.

[COPY RIGHT SECURED.]

9 7 8 3 3 3 7 8 7 7 6 4 4